RAS JAH STRENGTH PRESENTS...

THE STROKE OF
MY WRIST

A WORLD OF WORDS GELLED
INTO A BODY OF THOUGHTS

BY: The Luv Dactur (The Physician)

SOLOMON & MAKEDA INC.

Ras Jah Strength Presents...

The Stroke of
My Wrist

A WORLD OF WORDS GELLED INTO A BODY OF THOUGHTS

The Luv Dactur (The Physician)

LOVE

An emotion that's standing on the cliff of your thoughts
Awaiting to dive into the unconditional pool of another's
heart.

A feeling filled with sensations that calls for you to know
them forever, Like the boat of love that anchor its love in
any type of weather.

A vision within the mind that sets the state as so the eye
can see, what love looks like upon the face when its soul
is finally complete.

An unconditional feeling that will have ran its course if it
were to ever become a condition, a state of being,
undoing each and every emotion and beautiful sorted out
feeling.

EST. 07.23.14

NATRUAL LOVE

As the symphony of pouring rain drummed its recital against the land and earth, the rain drops of tears fell to the compassionate scene between man and woman that burned.

The union of man and woman is the beautiful bow of love, romantically fulfilling their compassion of the melodic sounds from the above.

The moans and cries of fulfilling compassionate pleasures, echoes throughout the fields of emotions where they have all gathered.

Awaiting in anticipation to fall from the cliff of passion, Into the awaiting pool of ecstasy filled satisfaction. (Natural Love)

EST. 07.20.13

TRUE LOVE

Sits up on the balcony of your mind peering over its
cliff,

Wondering will you be there to catch it if it were to
ever slip.

Like when two hearts become one that seems
impossible to become undone,

who can bear such an ache when love takes off and
run.

True love, a special feeling that can't be defined with
words,

for in the home of your heart is where such special
words are heard.

EST.11.02.12

LOVE

Is something special although it is somehow taken for granted,

and when one tried to perfect it no one can understand it.

It is something like a flower that you must nourish and water

in order to see it bud, like when emotions turn into feeling and

the heart beats with each pulse.

It is something unconditional out of the realm of thought,

For to grasp it is to let go and to fall without being caught.

EST.11.17.12

OPEN HEART SERGERY (ON A BROKEN HEART)

Pieces of love were scattered all over the floor of emotion,

even the window of love had suffered a deep crack after being left open.

Aches-and-pains were all huddled in a corner not sure of what to do,

while feelings came up with an idea that they all would be sure to pursue.

The idea was to gather each and every scattered piece of love,

then so ever carefully piece their battered bodies back together as one.

Next, they'd allow Aches-and-Pains to guide them through this pile of mixed emotions, as so Feelings could detect where each piece of love should go.

After Aches-and-Pains had exhausted themselves from such emotional handwork, Feelings then put the finishing touches

on it-by filling it up with enough love until it was about to burst.

Now that love has been fully restored-I assure you that

it'll be in no rush to start over in a hurry,

for no one likes the Aches-and-Pains,

nor the Feelings of an Open-heart Surgery.

EST.07.24.14

For: A WOMAN WITH A BROKEN HEART

Her thoughts are carried safely throughout the halls of her feminine cranium,

as the hands of her emotions sets out to resuscitate their lives by all means to somehow save them.

The window of her eyes are like that of drawn blinds,

for where there was once a glee that shined a coldness unheard of has taken its place as the reflection of her life.

The broken and shattered pieces that once made up the heart of such a beautiful woman, are carefully pieced back together by the hands of a man that really loves her.

So know that each of your heart felt aches, and mind shivering pains, will not go unnoticed by the caring eyes of such a man that isn't responsible for making you feel such a way.

EST.08.03.14

THE BROKEN HEART OF A WOMAN

Emotions of sculptured affections gathered together in perfect harmony, now shattered into pieces and ready for combat like that of an army.

As an avalanche of pain pours into the pit of her heart, it erupts from the ache with tears of lava that race down her face with no means to stop.

As an aftermath, this woman's soul is then filled with glacial ash,

and lifeless As death itself by the look of her glacial facial mask.

A cascade of emotional pain tells a story to the audience of life, about The Broken Heart of a Woman...the pain equivalent to that of being cut with a knife.

EST.03.05.14

A LONELY WOMAN

Allow me to take the hands of your thoughts into those of my own,

freeing you from the stronghold of loneliness and its intentions of never letting you go.

Allow me to pull back the curtains of your eyes, as to allow the rays of the sun to reflect

upon a beauty that no longer has to hide.

Allow me to perform open-heart surgery upon that of your own,

where no scar tissue will be visible and only an incision will mark the place where your pain once roamed.

A BROKEN HEART

Endless waves of emotions flow throughout the ocean of her heart, as the boat of love sets sail with the emotions of another as her feelings start to depart.

Tear-drops of rain falls from the window of her soul, As the flood-gates of heartache and pain she could no longer hold.

Within the chambers of her mind all thoughts have lost their sense of direction, for it was like committing suicide when they jump for nobody would listen.

The warmth within her emotions has turned cold for the blanket of love has been torn apart, abandoned like a lost soul with no one to turn to with a broken heart.

EST: 10.05.13

A BROKEN HEART

The doorway of the lips where each carefully chosen work must travel, is unlocked by the key within the tongue of its, thus master.

The listening ear awaits to take hold of such words that are spoken, in the moment of anticipation such words disappear as if a magical hocus-pocus. The perimeter of the heart is then filled with mixed emotions, enduring the war of love although transfixed by this unspoken notion.

The dagger of sacrifice is then taken into the hands of the heart, as a self-inflicted wound becomes the aftermath of A Broken Heart.

EST: 01.17.15

A RICH AND FAMOUS WOMAN

For her beauty is often mistaken for the hands of an artist's perfect picture,

as the pain within her eyes tells a story of a hurtful adventure.

As her emotions stand upon the cliff of her thoughts in anticipation of suicide, tears begin to avalanche down her face as a warning sign.

Lost in the beauty of her very presence her aches some how goes unnoticed,

For this is a story of A Rich and Famous Woman- told by the hands of a poet that doesn't even know her.

EST: 01.17.15

THE WOMAN

She is the root, river and route to all life upon this beautiful universe,

The beauty in what takes two when life calls for you to include it with her.

She is like a strong stem upon its petals that tickles your nostrils when inhaled into your nose.

She is the author of love written upon the tablet of all hearts,

the heart-beat within her bosom where one rest their head is the home where all love starts.

She is the tear within the eye and the pain within the ache, a blessing in disguise when all else failed you on your darkest of all days.

She is equivalent to that of the lioness that hunts the king of the jungle, nonchalantly roaming through life with mankind at her beck and call patiently awaiting to come running to her.

She gracefully remains an unsolved mystery that has yet To have been solved since the beginning of time,

Like the great pyramids of Egypt she has been studied but not duplicated by the hands of mankind.

EST: 01.10.14

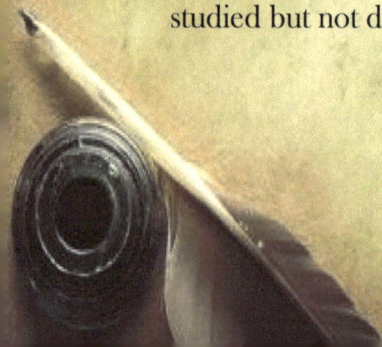

A WOMAN'S HEART

A WOMAN'S HEART

Is where all love derived from in the beginning of time,
for within such an emotional chamber of feelings inhaled
their first breath of this life.

A WOMAN'S HEART

Knew no aches nor pains outside of beautiful and
miraculous acts of birth, a pain that she was created to
endure and as an aftermath another life was born upon
the earth.

A WOMAN'S HEART

Would soon be faced with finding its way through the
world of sin, a place so cold where the blanket of her love
is removed and the warmth within it shall never be known
again.

A WOMAN'S HEART

Is said to be as fragile as the fine Vases of China, and
when it has been broken lines of aches paints her
beautiful face as if to remind her.

A WOMAN'S HEART

> *Dieu Vous garde <God keep you>

NOTHING LIKE A WOMAN

The way she thinks makes a difference in all conversations, for when the topic is about pain there's no need for words as a story is being told upon a many different beautiful faces.

The pupil of her eyes adjusts to the level of love that she sees each day,

for her heart has been broken before and knows when love is blind it can easily lead you astray.

Although she's metaphorically compared to all things that man loves, she's been around since the beginning of time and is historically by all means the portal that all men came from.

BEING AWAY FROM A WOMAN

A feeling that words couldn't possibly put into meaning, for each ache is far more greater than that of a break-up when you find-out that your lover is cheating.

You begin to think of her for what she is really worth, your time-understanding and all things that you neglected of her that made her hurt.

She makes a man want to piece her heart back together that was broken by someone else, for being away from a woman is like being on a stranded island screaming for help!!!

THE FEMININE BLANKET
(WHEN IT'S COLD OUTSIDE)

As winter tip-toe's throughout the night the cold wind blows slowly, in the warmth of many homes a many men and women are holding each other closely.

The beautiful sounds of oneness could be heard throughout the room with the listening ear, performed like that of a perfect piece orchestrated with a precision debonair.

Ecstasy has ran it course on the rise of its highest peak, as they jumped hand-in-hand from the cliff of love into a total exhausted silent sleep.

Wrapped as one in the beautiful bow of love like a cinnamon bracelet, with her bosom pressed against his back and her thigh thrown across his waist Keeping him warm with her feminine blanket.

EST: 01.19.14

HER FEMININE BLANKET

 As the cycle of nature seasons into the winter climate, the body of mankind seeks the warmth that only a woman is able to provide him with.

As the beautiful bow of man and woman is tied into a passionate knot, a beautiful love song is then orchestrated as his hands keys in on her passionate spots.

Her breaths are then deeply taken as he gyrates then thrust his hips into her feminine – inner-folds, as their bodies simultaneously applaud each time they mold.

As an aftermath of fulfilled passion exhaustion is giving in its replacement, as he then covers his body with her thighs and the warmth from Her Feminine Blanket.

EST: 01.19.14

WHEN OUR LIPS MET

It was like that of a blind date, with me not knowing how the sweetness of your lips would taste.

As we edged on to seal the fullness of such a beautiful kiss, my heart began to race as unidentified signals were being sent throughout it.

At such a point-time and moment one would think that I was the subject of weakness,

but I think it's safe to say that all that I wanted was a kiss filled with your sweetness.

I must say as a compliment in words with the safety of them not being caught-up in a net, the softness of your lips told a story when our lips met.

THE PERFECT TONGUE KISS

Simultaneous breaths are taken as the cleavage of the woman's bosom drowns the eyes down into its beautiful passage, as the mountain of her beautiful flesh heaves like that of sweet fruits upon loose branches.

The strong arms of the man envelopes her feminine being into its comforts, while lovingly touching the softness of her lips it's as if she wants to scream but he only receives a purr from her.

While pecking her with a trail of kisses up and down the nape of her neck, she begins to deeply exhale from the sensational feeling of each peck.

As his trail of kisses meet the anticipated agape mouth of her full-lips, they then engage into a brief tongue fight before she begins to pull and then suck on his. A beautiful union of man and woman as they bond together in a bow of oneness, as hypnotic stares are exchanged in the making of The Perfect Tongue Kiss.

EST: 07.22.14

THE LAST TIME

Words were spoken, feelings came alive and our emotions began to readjust, for love had entered into the home of our hearts with a set of spare keys unbeknownst to us.

We enjoyed the feelings of oneness as a token of love while in the company of each other, as we both lie breathless in a paralyzed state wrapped up in silk sheets with no covers.

We saw each other as a story was being told within the back of our minds, as we both know its hard to let go of what may come back for a second last time.

A SECOND LAST TIME- (THE SEQUEL)

To have patched up every hole within your heart and bandage each and every ache.

Give you the inspiration that there is no trial that your heart is not willing to face.

That is, until on that very day that special someone takes your heart and begins to toy with it, like that of a thief in the night peeking inside of those familiar holes with every intention of exploring it.

For revisiting the past of what you thought no longer existed, is like something that leaves you in awe more like a breath-taking experience.

A VALENTINE'S DAY LIKE NO OTHER

As you are enjoying this very special day I hope that you are able to fulfill its meaning,

like being showered with gifts and a candle-light dinner while sipping on a martini.

This is a day that was especially created for the woman to enjoy, as there is so many ways to explore it I just hope that you did in more ways than one.

You deserve to know that such thoughts could be created to reach out and tickle your heart, for we've only one life to live and what better place for laughter to serenade your sweetest parts.

While you're engaged with life in a full fledge earthly kiss, I felt that my carefully chosen words would be the shovel to unearth it with.

PIECES OF A LOST LOVE...BEAUTIFUL BETRAYAL... PERFECT PAIN

PIECES OF A LOST LOVE

Broken Pieces Of A Once Shattered Heart Were attentively pieced back together, with a maze within its glue that only he could undo the many stringed pieces meant to last forever.

BEAUTIFUL BETRAYAL

Struck by the blow of betrayal of an heartless imposter as if life was fading away, As a picture perfect mane of an illusional darkness encases his face.

PERFECT PAIN

An avalanche of shattered pieces of emotions that tumbled down into the pit of the heart, torn like that of an open wound of internal bleeding Creating blood-clogs.

EST: 05.03.14

STARTING OVER

Emotions for a journey with familiar routes to your destiny, for where there once were cautions signs there may be danger that awaits ahead of me.

Taking hold of the reins within my mind to guide me through the jungle of my thoughts, I see a woman along the way with a familiar face like that of the woman who crumbled my heart.

A woman that I don't want to face-so I take one last look over my departing shoulder, for I don't want to make the same mistake as this is the beautiful thing about starting over. PS the journey of Love: Now that I'm in the home of your heart you may lock the door and throw away the key...on the day that my heart can beat no more will be the day that I have decided to leave.

The End!

EST: 03.05.14

YOU'RE ALL I NEED

Nothing more could define the position of a wife like you have, it has been the very reason that you are my better half.

I thank GOD for every fiber within your body that you are made up of, a very special Kind that no other woman could take the place of.

You are the very essence of what it means, to say to you that you're ALL I NEED.

EST: 01.28.15

WHAT DO YOU DO?

When feelings for someone you barely know come alive, more like the doorway of my heart has cracked itself inviting this special someone inside.

Although the feelings of love isn't the wick that is lit, it awaits to avalanche down into the heart of another until its filled with it.

I question myself as to how it all took place out of the blue, for if the feelings are mutual, please, tell, me what do you do.

The End!

EST: 10.31.12

TIP-TOEING THROUGH YOUR FEMININE THOUGHTS

As I peek through the curtain of your thoughts, I am greeted by an emotion whose attention I have caught. Upon easing down from the ledge of the window, I noticed that this lone emotion had this steady tremble. So I took such a beautiful emotion by the hand and followed her lead, into the most beautiful forest of thoughtful trees. While tip-toeing down the pathway of friendship-I noticed how love was discussing signs of kinship. Then as I continued to travel along such a beautiful path – I noticed thoughts of my own that had made you laugh. Then this beautiful feminine emotion stopped dead in her tracks, as we had tip-toed upon a couple of your emotions discussing how they were planning to make me emotionally attached. It felt like an invasion but not when one enters before they knock, because in this case I was only Tip-toeing

Through Your Feminine Thoughts.

THROUGHOUT THIS LIFE

THROUGHOUT THIS LIFE

We shall come to face with the ups-and-downs of everyday life, but the beauty of it all-is when you can say "I forgive you" not once, but twice.

THROUGHOUT THIS LIFE

We'll make decisions and choices that shall place a wedge between us,

But that's only the work of the devil along with his four headed demons.

THROUGHOUT THIS LIFE

We'll reach out to those we love and miss just to see if they are alright,

Even go as far to make amends with a friend throughout this life.

EST: 08.30.14

BEAUTIFULLY BREAST FED

Through the period of gestation, a beautiful child is
born into the world, a mother's labor pains are soon
forgotten upon laying her eyes on her baby-boy or
beautiful baby-girl.
Her beautiful bosom becomes the softest pillow a
child shall every know,
The safe haven of peace as the child continues to
grow.
The beauty of a mother and child is like that of no
other, a picture that (God) framed within this life as
so a child can see how much their mother really
loves them.
Like the time that she takes out to reveal a beautiful
portion of her bosom, with a complimentary halo
and conical nipple for the child to suckle until its full
of.
The crescent realm of her soft bosom is a state-ment
of motherhood as the child take its fill, her caring
eyes watches lovingly as she feeds her child with her
ingredients (God) intimately instilled.

EST: 07.17.14

A MOTHER AND HER CHILD
(Plural Affection)

Within the safe haven of her stomach where Her Child is conceived,

The love of a Mother is poured into Her Child with each bite of food that she eats.

The beauty within the lifeline of each breath that her child breathes,

Is equivalent to that of a beautiful music with the sounds of Her Child's each heartbeat.

On the day that Her Child is born – as an aftermath of the miracle of birth that has taken place, tears of joy avalanches down the beauty of Mothers Lovely face.

As the eyes of Her Child longs for no other as to make it smile, you will have experienced the love of A Mother and Her Child.

EST: 09.26.14

THE SYMPHONY OF ALL LIFE

Composed to assure us that life awaits for us each
day, O how we anticipate to hear the beauty of such
harmony that is played.

Throughout the course of day a many people are at
peace because of such a musical work of art, for to
know such a sound is the beauty of how all life starts.

As a child rests upon its mother's bosom to such
pleasingly lyrics,

the life within the child is dancing in a dream filled
with rhythmic.

For we were created to only live once as our hearts
beat slowly throughout our life, O what music to the
ears composed by (God) the symphony of all life.

EST: 09.18.13
(Day before my mother's B-day)

THE BEAUTY OF A WOMAN

Strands of feminine hair encases her beautiful face, as rays of the sun reflect off the pupils of her eyes like that of a beautiful day.

Her beautiful nose suspends freely, quite like that of an oval cliff, above the beautiful realm of her succulent and suctorial lips.

The swan of her slender neck tower's over the wall of her beating heart, pulsating like that of a stream of love filled with sweetness in its deepest parts.

The fullness of her bosom is like that of a mountain tip, with a valley of cleavage running deep down into its softest parts.

The beauty of her tummy is how it waterfalls down into her feminine waist, that, in turn, avalanches down into a set of hips and thighs of perfect shape.

Her cute calves gel down into a set of awesome ankles, as her beautiful pedicured feet holds her down like that of a ship with an anchor.

A PERFECT PICTURE OF A WOMAN:
(Pretty in the face and thick in the waist)

The countenance of her beauty is encased by strands of loose hair, accentuated by a set of soothing eyes that reflects upon that of your own as to show you that she cares.

The beauty of her nose suspends over the realm of her succulent lips, as they part at liberty for her instructive tongue and its soft tip.

The business of her bosom that makes for her pillow-like flesh, is a safe haven for all that have at some point laid their head to rest.

The thickness of her waist that avalanches down into a set of succulent thighs, is a combination of her genetics and the thickness of her bones that she carries with pride.

The beauty of such a woman is the fullness of her figure and how her dimples have settled into place, A Perfect Picture of a Woman that's pretty in the face and thick in the waist.

EST: 12.16.14

THE CURTAINS OF LOVE

Awaits for two souls to merge into that of one, for the stage is being set for an audience who only have dreams that are of love.

The unforgettable breath-taking moments of love at its best, serenading a love tone to your heart as it dances within your chest.

A many have taken a peek but only a few have drawn them open, for what lies behind these curtains when you're in love there's no need for words to be spoken.

HURT

Being apart of another to equal that of a whole, is easier said then done, when given someone else's heart to hold

The choices that are made creates the road that is paved, down into the inner most parts of the heart where her love has started to decay.

Thinking of a life together as one upon this very earth, in the beginning seemed to be beautiful until love stung and began to really hurt.

EST: 11.01.12

A COMPOSED ONENESS

The motion of the wind penetrated the parts between our fingers as if held in place to welcome the breeze of its tickle.

As if amused by its blanket of painted chills like a promise ring of nature.

As the gates of the hands close from the binding interlock of oneness the wind is suffocated into the cave of togetherness.

EST: 11.11.17

LOVE UNTOLD

The window of the eyes opens to the smile of a child born into this world

The heart of the child pounds upon the doorway of its mother's awaiting for her to welcome the much-needed rest upon her pillowed bosom.

The perimeter of nourishment barricades the child within a nest of a mother's cultivation.

EST: 11.11.17

ORGANIC COMMUNICATION

The lungs exert its compressors. The power-driven belts of the esophagus pipes escalator stairway upward. The crosspieces of the tongue are ascended into a takeoff sprint on to its diving board tip. Spiraling precipitously into the canal of the eardrum. Plunging into an anticipated splash within the pool of your thoughts.

EST: 11.11.17

RECIPROCATIVE ROMANCE

Oral warfare filled with tongue knife fights.
Suffocating intakes of one another moans of ecstasy.
Paste budded nipples tip toe across the mountain of
masculinity. Wipeout waves of flesh applaud the
incoming storm of passionate strokes. Suction cup
walls of flesh encircles an ithyphallic liberating its
scrotum capacity in a paralleled bow of waterfall
reciprocative romance.

EST: 11.11.17

ORGANIC MAYHEM

The brain took offense at the way the heart beat.
The lungs are upset because esophagus pipe is
holding its breath. The bladder is pissed off
completely. The stomach thinks everyone is full of it.
The kidney can't see what's funny about any of this.
The heart is laughing because this is an inside joke to
him as he knows how everybody feel.

EST: 11.11.17

HOLDING ON TO JUST ONE WOMAN

The jealously orbiting within her ogled glance was ephemeral. The beautiful adjacent of man accompanied by a woman was unpleasantly dreaded. An assault to the core of the heart. Ridicule to the lonesome and insatiably craved to the abandon.

Tunnel vision was the cause of arthritis within the hands of the eyes. Faithfully with the focal attentiveness of her captivating beauty. A tiresome honor of loyal integrity. An exhaustive declaration of explanation as to not offend the opposing party. The gravitation of greediness to the countering unknown rival. An allegiance and pledge of a combined duality of warring fasten faithfulness.

EST: 11.11.17

WALKING WITH LOVE

There upon the mountain of the heart huddled in the shadows of pain are marked emotions. The rumor of love's return has spread as if an epidemic. All whom have experienced raw aches and pain have taken their place plan to observe love in its great measures. The residue of such an ache shivers throughout the soul of each emotion. A watchfulness considered to be that of a canny eyed old soul absorbs love's every motion.

Smiles that start in the corner regions are examined to see if they are genuinely contagious. It must have taken its affect as the warmth can be felt throughout the community of emotions all in hopes of this feeling to withstand the test of all four corners of its unconditional dimensions. As love prepares to depart for the timing of the day with intentions of returning to take up where it left off is gut-wrenching nerve wrecking.

As the love they had emotionally encountered makes its way in the bubble of trust they watch until its silhouette fades into the distance. Then and only then does mix signals begin to trigger as mixed emotions take sides form the after effects of the past experience. As the tug-of-war parades throughout the heart a warmth settles amongst them all as the boomerang of returned love awakes them from this emotional frenzy that carried on without notion of the morrow peeking over the horizon like the shadows of the radiant sun. Love envelopes the emotional party with assuring blankets of trust and truths as the attempt to break free of what they have longed for...A walk with love.   EST: 11.11.17

A LONESOME FEELING

Settled comfortably within the palm of a plush chair. Thoughts of anticipation travel the distance of your bold heart and exhilarating mind. Ogled glances make their way to the window of your thoughts. Doubt climbs upon the balcony of you heart. An orchestra of impatient fingers drum unrhythmically upon the arm of the chair as if a snare. The pupil of the eyes absorb the room as that of a predator its prey only seeking that of a familiarity of a lovely countenance. The unbearable impacting pressures of anticipation threaten to break the damn within the heart. The cubes of ice began to abandon their form as they had lost their cool. Just as the thought of canceling the moment crossed the bridge of your mind a feminine silhouette graces the cozy entrance of the restaurant. Blanketed by the darkness of the dim lit room she stands motionless as if uninterested.

AM I ALIVE?

I inhale and exhale but I truly do not experience its full reciprocative tunnel travel. I sort through the endless thoughts of what is said-discarded or stored within the memory bank. I hear the rhythm while the mechanics of the body flow. The core of a feeling peeks from behind the curtain of the heart as I slowly draw the curtains. I am the life within often ignored until the hairs upon your skin take a stand, thus only then I shall awaken from a stage of dormancy.

EST: 11.11.17

HUMANLY ROYAL

The castle of thought settled impeccably imminent upon the rooftop of the courageous countenance. The pupil of the eyes watched from the balcony of sight. As the realm of the nose nest perfectly beneath with clandestine oval passages. The beautiful crevice of the lips lies agape with a crafted curtain of ivory that can be seen under the perfect moonlight. The tower of the neck holds the nape of ivory crosspieces of the Queen's nocturnal rendezvous. A cozy bosom bush with halo walls of sacred budding roses encases a romantic cleavage waterfall. Cascading from its cliff down into the chamber of the King's heart creating an aqua window for the eyes of his Queen.

EST: 11.11.17

For your Publishing Needs...